Pebble® Plus

GREAT ASIAN AMERICANS

Patsy Mink

by Stephanie Cham

CAPSTONE PRESS
a capstone imprint

Pebble Plus is published by Capstone Press,
1710 Roe Crest Drive, North Mankato, Minnesota 56003
www.mycapstone.com

Cataloging-in-Publication Data is available from the Library of Congress website.
Names: Cham, Stephanie, author.
Title: Patsy Mink / by Stephanie Cham.
Description: North Mankato, Minnesota : Pebble Plus, an imprint of Capstone
  Press, 2018. | Series: Great Asian Americans
Identifiers: LCCN 2017044058 (print) | LCCN 2017046523 (ebook) | ISBN 9781515799757 (eBook)
  PDF) | ISBN 9781515799542 (hardcover) | ISBN 9781515799696 (pbk.)
Subjects: LCSH: Mink, Patsy T., 1927-2002. | Legislators—United States—Biography—
  Juvenile literature. | Women legislators—United States--Biography—Juvenile literature.
  Legislators—Hawaii—Biography—Juvenile literature. | Women legislators—Hawaii—
  Biography—Juvenile literature. | United States. Congress—Biography—Juvenile literature.
  Women athletes—Government policy—United States—Juvenile literature. | United States.
  Education Amendments of 1972. Title IX—Juvenile literature. | Asian Americans—
  Biography—Juvenile literature. | Asian American women—Biography—Juvenile literature.
Classification: LCC E840.8.M544 (ebook) | LCC E840.8.M544 C47 2018 (print) |
DDC 328.73/092 [B] —dc23
LC record available at https://lccn.loc.gov/2017044058

Editorial Credits
Abby Colich, editor; Juliette Peters and Charmaine Whitman, designers;
Morgan Walters, media researcher; Kathy McColley, production specialist

Photo Credits
ASSOCIATED PRESS, 17, JOE MARQUETTE, 21; Getty Images: Bettmann, 5, 19; Shutterstock:
Attitude, design element throughout, Eric Baker, 7, j avarman, (pattern) design element
throughout, Jannis Tobias Werner, 11, popular, design element throughout, Theodore Trimmer,
15; The Image Works: TopFoto, 9; Wikimedia: U.S. Congress, Cover, 13

Note to Parents and Teachers

The Great Asian Americans set supports standards related to biographies.
This book describes and illustrates the life of Patsy Mink. The images support
early readers in understanding the text. The repetition of words and phrases
helps early readers learn new words. This book also introduces early readers
to subject-specific vocabulary words, which are defined in the Glossary
section. Early readers may need assistance to read some words and to use
the Table of Contents, Glossary, Read More, Internet Sites, Critical Thinking
Questions, and Index sections of the book.

Printed and bound in the USA.
010771S18

Table of Contents

Early Life

Patsy Mink was born in 1927.

She grew up in Hawaii.

Her grandparents had moved there

from Japan. Patsy loved to read.

She wanted to be a doctor one day.

1927
born on December 6
in Paia, Hawaii

Patsy did well in school.

She ran for student president.

She was the first girl to run

for student office. She won.

1944

graduates from
high school

Patsy went to high school in Maui, Hawaii.

School Challenges

Patsy went to college. She had to live in separate housing. It was for nonwhite students. Patsy knew this was not fair. She got others to write letters. The school ended the rule.

1948
graduates
from college

1927   1944

Patsy still wanted to be a doctor.

She tried to go to medical school.

At the time few women were let in.

A teacher said she should study law.

Patsy went to law school.

1948–1951
goes to law
school at the
University of
Chicago

Patsy finished law school. She looked

for a job. Many people did not give

jobs to women. No one gave her a job.

She began her own law office.

She taught law too.

1953
begins own
law office

13

Work in Politics

In 1956 Patsy ran for congress
in Hawaii. She won. She was the first
Asian American in Hawaii's congress.
Soon she ran for Hawaii's senate.
She won that race too.

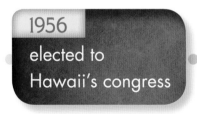
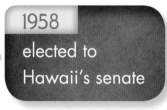

1956
elected to
Hawaii's congress

1958
elected to
Hawaii's senate

1927   1944   1948   1951   1953

Hawaii's congress met at Iolani Palace in the 1950s.

In 1960 Patsy gave a big speech.

It was on TV. People around

the country heard it. She said everyone

is equal. Lawmakers heard her words.

They chose to work for more civil rights.

1960
gives speech at Democratic
National Convention

Patsy ran for U.S. Congress in 1964.
She won. She was the first nonwhite
woman in Congress. In 1972
she helped write a new law.
It helped give women equal rights.

1964
elected to
U.S. Congress

1972
helps write Title IX
of the Education
Amendments

1927   1944   1948   1951   1953   1956   1958   1960

Patsy left Congress in 1977.

She did other work. She went back

in 1989. She became sick in 2002.

She soon died. Her work for

equal rights is remembered today.

1989
returns to Congress

2002
dies

1927 1944 1948 1951 1953 1956 1958 1960 1964 1972

Glossary

civil rights—the rights that all people have to freedom and equal treatment under the law

congress—an official meeting of representatives from various nations, states, or colonies

law—a rule made by the government that must be obeyed

lawmaker—an elected official who makes laws

medical—having to do with the practice of medicine

senate—one of the two houses of Congress that makes laws

student office—a group of students chosen to represent their classmates

Read More

Cane, Ella. *The U.S. House of Representatives*. Our Government. North Mankato, Minn.: Capstone, 2014.

Ferguson, Melissa. *U.S. Government: What You Need to Know*. Fact Files. North Mankato, Minn.: Capstone, 2018.

Oachs, Emily Rose. *Hawaii: The Aloha State*. Exploring the States. Minneapolis, Minn.: Bellwether Media, 2014.

Internet Sites

Use FactHound to find Internet Sites related to this book.

Visit *www.facthound.com*

Just type in 9781515799542 and go.

Super-cool stuff! Check out projects, games and lots more at
www.capstonekids.com

Critical Thinking Questions

1. Why did Patsy go to law school?
2. It was not easy for Patsy to go to school or get a job she wanted because she was a woman. If Patsy were alive today, would things be different for her? Explain why or why not.
3. What is one way Patsy helped women?

Index